HERE.

HERE. Copyright © 2022 By Junya Hatta.
All rights reserved.
No part of this book may be reprodouced in any form
without written permission from the author.

Design & Layout by Rachel Clift.

ISBN: 978-1-7780576-0-1

HERE.

by

Junya Hatta

2022
NEW YORK :: TORONTO

Acknowledgments

For Kenta

FOR ALWAYS BEING HERE

For Alfred

FOR YOU TAUGHT ME LOVE.

NOW IT'S MY TURN TO TEACH SOMEONE ELSE.

For Ms. Showers

FOR YOU'VE ALWAYS SHOWERED ME

WITH PRAISE AND ENCOURAGEMENT.

DEAR READER,

We believe what we are looking for is never in the present, but somewhere out *there*. But, when we get *there*, where ever *there* may be, we aren't satisfied. "This has to be a mistake," we say to ourselves. So, we keep going, finding a new *there* to chase. So, every *here* merely becomes a pit stop for a *there*. We pass by these moments forgetting that a *here* has value as well – maybe even a value that far surpasses a *there*. We are never happy *here* because we always want to be *there*.

But what would life look like if we were *here*? If we lived *here*?
If we loved *here*?
Although there is a time and place for a *there*, it shouldn't come
at the cost of the *here*.

Because,
HERE,
is the only place we truly live.

Best,
JUNYA HATTA

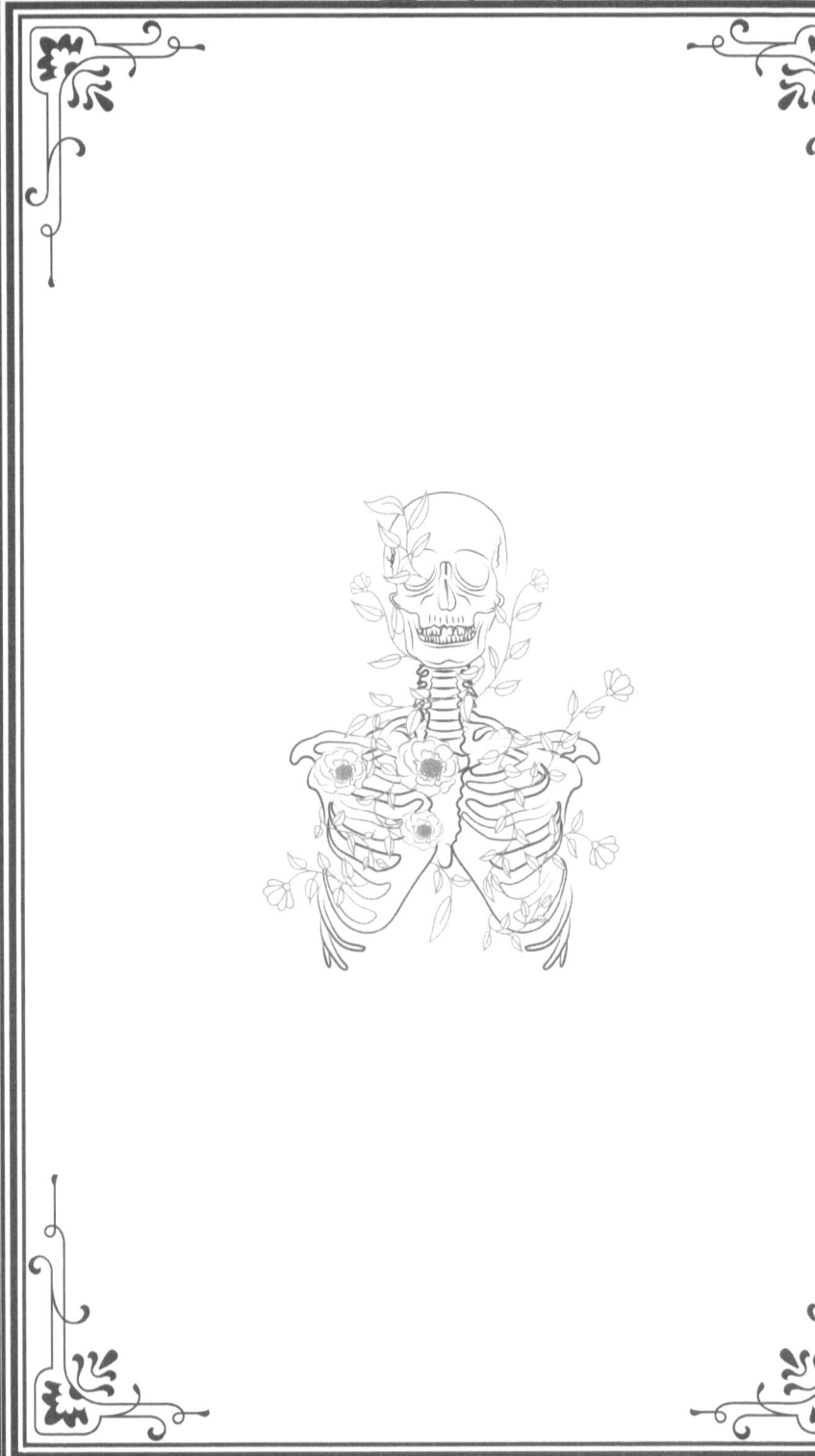

HERE.

When you feel the world is better off without you.

Remember

someone's world would be lost without you.

Junya Hatta

HERE.

If I tell myself to be grateful for just one day.
If I tell myself to be patient for one more day.
If I tell myself to be happy for one day.
That day would be today.
Because today is only one day, yet today is forever.

Junya Hatta

HERE.

I'm somewhere between the person I want to be,
and the person that I am.
A part of me that I want to keep,
and another I want to change.
The middle is where I reside,
but in the middle,
is where I fall or rise.
Respect the middle,
for it will be,
your destiny.

Junya Hatta

HERE.

Remember the person you are today,

for they won't be here for long.

By tomorrow you will be someone new thanks to you.

The you that you were,

The you that was hurt.

The you that you stated you hated and berated,

With self-inflicting statements,

But somehow found a way to make it.

You made it because a part of you didn't break,

And if it did, it was supposed to anyways.

Remember the person you are today,

Because then you will see,

How far you've come when you thought you strayed.

Remember the person you are today,

For they won't be here for long.

LOVE DANGEROUSLY

Love you are dangerous.

Dangerously good.

Love dangerously -

in a world who fears being moved.

HERE.

You are my favourite song,

the one stuck in my head.

The one I hum along

when I should be thinking of something instead.

So even if you are gone,

I wanted you to know,

to me,

you never really left.

HERE.

If I had a flower for every time you made me smile,
I would have a garden.
And when I'm angry, I would sit in the middle,
and forget why my heart was hardened

Junya Hatta

HERE.

ONLY LOVE REMAINS

After the hurt.

After the pain.

After everything.

When all else is gone,

Only love remains.

HERE.

The wild is such a beautifully dangerous place.

Where everything was built on the destruction of another.

So be wild with me.

Let your love destroy who I was,

so I can be built into something free.

HERE.

I want to thank my sorrows of yesterday,

So, I can plan a better tomorrow starting today.

I never would've made it this far,

Until I knew,

All hurts eventually turn to scars.

Junya Hatta

I WANT TO HOLD YOUR HAND

When I hold your hand,

I don't just hold your hand.

I hold your trust,

that everything will be fine with our love.

I hold your dreams,

that our future is brighter than it seems.

I hold you,

and everything that you offer me.

So when I hold your hand,

I don't just hold your hand.

I hold all of you,

until it becomes all of me.

HERE.

I never want to forget and take my future for granted —

because some of us don't get one.

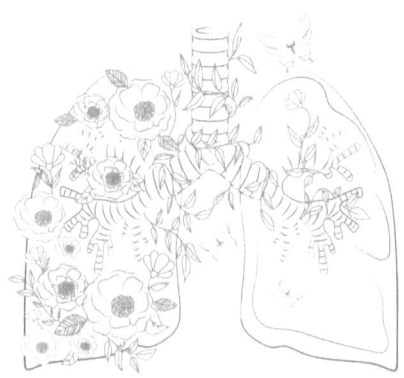

Junya Hatta

MY WALK HOME

You are my beautiful worry - my favourite handful

like the way I fear a dandelion would be trampled.

I would love to uproot you and replant you somewhere safe,

but in doing so, kill the exact beauty that makes you great.

For you survive in the most desolate place with such grace,

always finding a way.

So, I will love you from afar and watch you grow,

because you are my favourite handful,

but stronger than I would ever know.

HERE.

Love is wanting my way and then throwing it away.

Because with you,

my selfishness has nowhere to stay.

Junya Hatta

I WANT TO BE POOR WITH YOU PT. I

I want to wake up early in the morning and make you breakfast.
Pour cereal into the same bowls we ate ramen from the previous night.
Pour water into mine and all the milk into yours.
Because that's what you've always done for me before.

HERE.

Your life is measured in time.

But valued in love.

HERE.

We sometimes forget,

Life is a once in a lifetime experience.

Junya Hatta

HERE.

Why we are friends:

You taught me love is a waterfall that fills,

My heart until it spills.

Junya Hatta

HERE.

To dream is to be human.

Anything less

is just a body in movement.

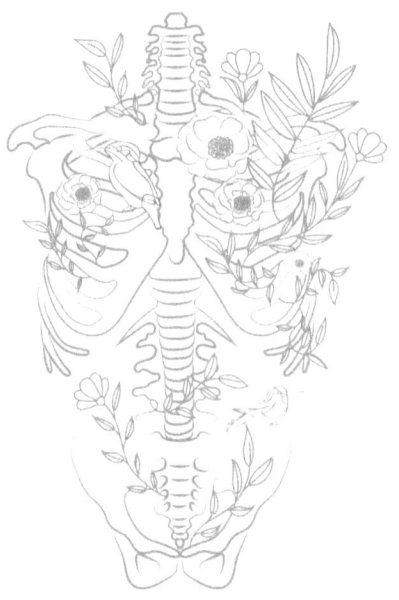

Junya Hatta

HERE.

CONDO #536

The story goes...

Good girl, gone bad

Crooked world, wrong path

Bright future, but a long past

She used to smile at the little things and laugh out loud but now

Tears stream down her face and splash to the ground

She looks up, "God if you are real where are you now?

How do you expect me to believe in something

that's not been around?"

You see,

She hangs around with her ex who is obsessed with,

Beating her and having sex and texting his exes

saying he's got to go see his next "friend".

Her life is a mess and always restless

So, one day she goes and confesses,

"I can't be with you anymore. I learned my lessons.

You say you love me, but I'm always stressed and

Junya Hatta

HERE.

I'm going to pack my bags and leave the condo,

So, don't look for me because I won't be here by tomorrow".

Then, he grabs her hand, but he's too powerful.

Darkness.

She wakes up

Blood and tears smearing her make up.

Lying in a hospital bed,

she could have been possibly dead.

A man in her view, she asks, "Who are you? I don't even know".

"I'm the neighbor living down below.

I heard a noise and came to your door

and a man holding a bottle with bad intentions

came at me and I prevented

him hitting you and now he's arrested

I'm an undercover cop, he'll never touch you again. This is the end.

You are safe".

She closed her eyes and prayed, "God I'm sorry I doubted,

you never disowned me.

You've been looking out for me - not from above, but below me"

Junya Hatta

HERE.

The world will see you for your status.

Love will see you for your potential.

HERE.

I wanted you.

Then I needed you.

So I let you go,

because I needed to.

HERE.

I can sing in the rain and dance in the storm,
Because I have survived it before.

Junya Hatta

SUPERNOVA

You remind me of something broken, yet something new.

You mix elegance with a supernova

Where the universe begins.

So, when I look at you

You remind me of a feeling.

Of something I always was needing.

But I'm here in this moment

And I want to enjoy it.

Because tomorrow isn't promised for

You and I.

HERE.

THE ROSE FROM THE CONCRETE

My words are a seed of love and I plant them along my way,
hoping some land in the paths I decide to stray.
By the side of the road, to the paths high and the low.
Even if the winds blow away what I decide to lay,
may they find another home in the ground
of someone else's place.
Even if people on the paths kick or crush,
the little seeds of my spoken love,
may I continue to speak freely and lay seeds softly,
in all places and paths,
hoping a garden will exist when the world is filled with concrete.

Junya Hatta

HERE.

The irony of love is that it'll cost you everything,

Yet you lose nothing.

HERE.

1 DAY

You say some day, the one day will arrive.
The one day you'll finally feel alive.
But please let today be the one day you would do what you said,
because one day you won't have some days left.

MATTHEW 18: 1-2

I am unsure if my life will ever lead to something great.
But hopefully in the small acts of love,
maybe the world will be a better place.
Maybe my life will never be the way I envisioned,
because my life was meant for something different.
Because greatness is temporary, but love continues to live,
Reborn, reformed,
from ordinary to beauty to exist.

HERE.

There's something beautiful about feeling sadness,
But in the end finding joy.
Being grateful for what happened,
And not consumed by the void.

Junya Hatta

HERE.

She asked, "What makes life beautiful?"
I said, "You make life beautiful,"
"So go
make life beautiful."

Junya Hatta

CHASING PACIFIC WINDS

From the edge of the west,

I stand looking over.

The waves spider up shores,

Leaving a seafoam web.

Like a flock perching on a shaded branch,

The Pacific wind blows and mist nestles in my hair.

Our paths will cross and I will wave

Like kelp swayed by the undercurrent.

Junya Hatta

HERE.

NOVEMBER 17, 2021

I try and find ways to hold you back because although you moved on and are happy with someone else, I still feel like I'm missing a part of myself. I know you're happy and that's what matters the most, so, if I ever accidentally fall in love and try to draw you close, please push me away no matter how much I insist and persist that hope exists. Because I need to move on too even if the best part of me was always being with you. I lust for the warmth the way the summer breeze shakes the leaves, knowing fall is merely around the corner. For I yearn the warmth at least once more before the branches become bare, and you prepare for the early sunsets and as seasons forget, the cold will kill all the things that refuse to take refuge. I'm sorry if I feel so desperate, because my heart is broken and I'm just trying to hold onto what's left of it.

Junya Hatta

HERE.

BLOSSOMING TO ONE DAY BE REMEMBERED

Peaking slow over the horizon's night,
Love, you shined onto all that was concealed.
You sprouted my heart, seeds of passion like,
The heaven's rays warm blanketed lush fields.

For you I have loved, for you I have held,
Hand in hand like vines crawling on stone walls.
The palm of your hand which deep grooves were felt;
Our love like summer's night approaching fall.

A stranger among the smallest world of mine,
A dandelion seed floats through the air.
Perhaps the breeze gave way to me this sign,
To let go of her whom I feel to care.

I have chased the wind when the seasons changed.
Now I lay still ready for autumn rain.

Junya Hatta

NEW YORK

I used to hate the city.

Because it was way too busy.

Until I met you.

Because in a room full of people

it's like you're the only one with me.

HERE.

INSTASCAM INFLUENCERS

The world will sell you things to rob you of your value,

the one that you tried to find in yourself.

But then you tried to find it on a shelf.

Going store to store to explore,

things you never saw before,

the ones you can't afford, the ones you can't ignore,

because without it, people will see you as poor.

But what I hope is that one day you find,

something that the world cannot supply,

your worth in something more.

Junya Hatta

I WANT TO HOLD YOUR HAND

I want to hold your hand and lead you into adventure.

I want to hold your hand and just run.

To run away and as fast as we can.

Where are we going?

I have no plan.

I want to hold your hand as we jump off a cliff.

I want us to count to three, run, and jump on, "Go!"

Falling is scary, but less scary with you into the water below.

My feet may kick and move, but my arm is kept steady by you.

When we hit the water, I want to hold your hand

so we won't float away.

So, no matter what, never let me stray.

Even if it hurts, don't let go.

Because the pain of losing you is far worse than the pain

that my body may feel when I fall.

Junya Hatta

HERE.

I want to hold your hand when I go to sleep,
Because then I will feel safe and secure.
To pull me out of my nightmares and into your dreams.
I want to hold your hand to feel your pulse onto my wrists.
I want to feel the creases and have them overlap with mine like this.

I want to hold your love,
and never let go,
that's my only plan.

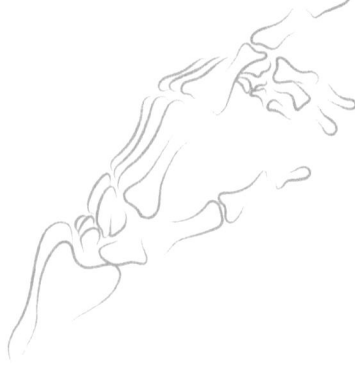

Junya Hatta

HERE.

Those that love deeply

Learn to live freely.

HERE.

Your arms hug me so tight,

It creases my shirts.

Your love, so strong,

Takes my soul,

And smooths out its edges.

Junya Hatta

I WANT TO BE POOR WITH YOU PT. II

When we go out,

I want to sit at a table by the window.

Where we can look out to all the apartments we can't afford.

Order only apps that we share and

sneak in wine from the store.

I want to hold your hand across the table and I want you

to hold my attention.

I want to waive the waiter down and he looks

in the opposite direction.

We'll probably be asked to leave so

an elderly well-dressed couple can sit.

Yeah, they may have more money and probably more class,

but we have our youth.

And I have someone to make today a memory of the past.

HERE.

3AM TEXTS IN WAHI

"What's wrong?"

"Nothing. I don't want to talk about it."

"Can I not talk about it with you?"

"Can you come over and not talk about now?"

"Yeah. I want to not talk about it with you any day."

HERE.

JUMP

I never want the fear of pain

To overshadow

The joy of love.

Junya Hatta

HERE.

The greatest lessons you learn is forgiveness.
Not only to others but to yourself.
Because forgiveness is the only thing that saves you,
from your self-created hell.

Junya Hatta

WE ARE ALL POETS

Words are powerful.

Love is powerful.

Speak words of love,

and you are unstoppable.

HERE.

Your life is beautiful and poetic.

That is why only a few truly get it.

THE BRIGHTSIDE OF THE MOON

After all these nights, I still think of you.

Maybe because the thoughts of you return like the moon.

Sometimes in full.

Sometimes only in parts.

Sometimes being hidden behind cloudy memories,

appearing for short periods of time inside of my heart.

So at night you are the thing that keeps me up,

I toss and turn, then look at you,

I can't sleep, yet I can't get enough.

HERE.

The question you should be asking isn't if other people
care about your dream,
but if your dreams
care about other people.

Junya Hatta

HERE.

I don't know if kindness is always the right answer,
but so far,
it has never been the wrong one.

HERE.

The sunny crisp

Of autumn leaves

Like my love

is falling free.

Seasons change

people change too.

Where the wind blows,

I will follow you.

Junya Hatta

HERE.

One day we will be reunited like

the bird perched on its favorite tree.

How the bees nestle into the pollen bed

of its favorite flower every spring.

What once a cold, deathlike season,

everything will be renewed,

even love.

Junya Hatta

HERE.

Her heart was an autumn tree holding onto the final leaf.

Before a wind of disbelief blew away her remaining piece.

But little does she know,

a time will come when everything will regrow.

So, when the winds blow, let it go,

the heart will be made whole,

in another season we have yet to reach.

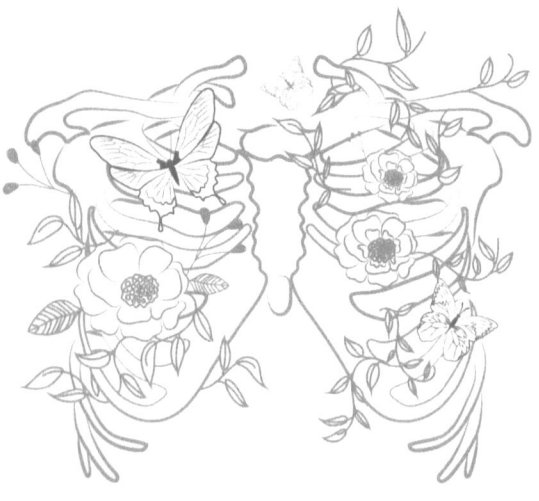

Junya Hatta

HERE.

You don't need to be fixed,

you need to be connected to what you were once before.

Before you were uprooted and taken to somewhere new,

somewhere not meant for you and deep down you knew.

You refused to refuse because you thought it was rude.

But fear not, for love will water your roots

and regrow all the things you lost,

to one day bloom even the beautiful things you forgot.

Junya Hatta

HERE.

I WANT TO BE POOR WITH YOU PT. III

I couldn't resist but I had to get her a gift.
I had to sell my favorite watch for cash,
To buy a charm she wanted but was always afraid to ask.
The next day, she opened the box, but couldn't help but laugh,
"Honey, I sold my bracelet don't be mad,
To get you the band for the watch you always flash."
Money is tight to the point of financial crisis,
But here I am, rich in love that is priceless.

Junya Hatta

HERE.

The song of the caged bird can sing so sweetly.

But the bird that is free, writes poetry in the sky.

HERE.

IT'S A LONG WAY HOME

Life will throw you more obstacles than medals.
It may not seem right until we reach the pinnacle.
Until then, we must look up - at the mountain top -
so one day we can look down.
Look down at the problems - the mountains -
we thought so large. The same ones we just
conquered.
That's what looking up does.

Junya Hatta

BRANCHES

Your words perch on me

like a bird in a tree.

You came with the breeze

and left with the leaves.

Then the air dips

several degrees,

And my branches freeze.

Yet

Deep down to my roots and out to my shoots,

I truly believe,

your words will return,

back home to me.

Junya Hatta

HERE.

SEASON II

I wish for you to experience every season of life.

To spring into it,

to fall for it.

To winter through the cold,

to one day feeling the heat of the moment.

Then once more, when the seasons begin,

each one bringing,

a memory from within.

To find love,

You must become it.

HERE.

BOOK MARKS

I used to collect the leaves that fell from the trees

and place them into my pocket.

I carry them home, press them into books,

and make bookmarks.

And every time I read, I open the pages and see,

how something that died,

was turned into something new,

something it wasn't designed to do,

yet perfectly fulfills the purpose,

and fills my heart,

more than any bookmark I got from you.

Junya Hatta

HOW BRAVE THE SEED IS

How brave the seed is.

Although buried deep underground,

literally crushed by the world,

it refuses to die,

yet come alive.

To grow, when the ground has thawed,

when all things were thought,

to be dead and never come back anymore.

Be like the seed.

Junya Hatta

HERE.

LIFE

Life is scary because anything can happen.

Life is beautiful because anything can happen.

Those that can handle painful goodbyes,
Will eventually encounter the most beautiful hellos.

HERE.

The fragility of life can only be combatted with the resiliency of faith.

Junya Hatta

HERE.

PERFECT

If everything was perfect,
life would be worthless.
For beauty is found in the flaws,
that were made into purpose.

HERE.

THE EQUATION

Life is the sum of the experiences,

the differences made in others,

the multiplication of joy, and

the division of worries.

Junya Hatta

MY EVERYTHING

What you give and how much when you have nothing,
defines your everything.

HERE.

> Maybe life is beautiful,
>
> not in spite of,
>
> but because of,
>
> the unusual.

Junya Hatta

HERE.

ROAD MAPS

At our age we are all searching the same thing –

we are searching for what we are searching for,

Not knowing exactly what we are looking for.

Maybe the search for what we are searching for starts with starting.

To take the step in a direction, in any direction.

From there, we sort of wander –

to let our curiosity do what it was always designed to do: take

the lead when logic can no longer.

And when we see glimpses where we feel alive,

Mixes of instances where are interests intersect

with purpose and drive,

Like a supernova of bliss.

Hold onto that moment and inch closer,

And nothing will be the same.

Junya Hatta

HERE.

IN ORDER

In order to be, you must do.
In order to do, you must think.
In order to think, you must feel.
In order to feel, you must care.
In order to care, you must love.
In order to love, you must be
Loved.

Junya Hatta

HERE.

THE A

I like to sit on the train and let the thoughts of you invade my brain.
Like where we first met in lower Manhattan
where I had a little too much and you came over to see what happened.

Maybe I said some things a little too wild, yet you were kind enough to smile.
Or near Midtown where we would walk around looking for murals to see,
because we both loved art but hated spending an entry fee.

Or the time in Brooklyn we walked over the bridge,
and we loved to call all the tourists a, "Fucking bitch."
Or how about that time we both wanted ramen? Which is often.
And we stood in line for a hell of a long time, but then got dollar pizzas instead.

But my favorite station is where we waited
for you to board your plane.
And I prayed for a miracle for your plane to be delayed,
knowing God always answers the prayers of lovers parting ways.

So, I took your hand and pulled you near and whispered into your ear,
"Please just give me one more day."
You smiled. I smiled. And we took off.

Junya Hatta

HERE.

We ran up escalators in the opposite direction,
rode the luggage carousel,
security looking for us, looking mad as hell.
We ate every sample and then tried on
every perfume at the duty free.
Although time was running low, I never felt love grow,
more than you being with me.

"Next stop 168th station..."
I stand up from my seat, when I hear the station name.
I exit the subway, but my mind still travels
down memory lane.

Junya Hatta

HERE.

MY DARK TWISTED FANTASY

I would rather argue with you than to be with someone else,
Because only you can walk with me through the fires of hell.
So instead of finding "love" with someone new,
I would rather find purpose again struggling with you.

HERE.

DEAR,

I lie in bed and write all these words to you.
Somehow, one day, hoping they can find a way to your eyes,
onto your tongue, and into your
being.
May these words brighten your sight, sweeten your taste,
and give your life more meaning.
But I'm sorry if my love notes are never neat,
because I always write the way that I speak.
Whenever I think of you, I ramble on and go on tangents,
and I feel like I have to tell you everything that happened.
For words are not simply words. They are me.
They are my entirety expressed through scribbles of poetry.
But these words would not be possible with you because
you make every thought beautiful – you make every line matter.
The few lines that I have are not enough to capture,
how your love deserves not letters,
but books with never ending chapters.
Read my words and let it enter your heart,
then, I will forever live with you until death do us apart.

Junya Hatta

THE PUER AETERNUS

I remember growing up,

I knew very little of the world because I never needed to.

Because I was naïve enough to believe I was surrounded by only good.

Each day, I began to learn the truth about the things I love,

Like how no one told me that all beautiful things will eventually die.

I asked my mother why this happens and she said these words,

"Sometimes 'life' happens,"

And this is a natural part of being a part of this earth.

How cruel nature is, but how much more humanity can transcend it.

How nature can be broken, but can't humanity be able to mend it?

But the more I looked at people, I slowly saw how much we aren't different.

How the beautiful things naturally fall into devasting existence,

Like there are sick people that don't get better,

Like how people who love each other don't end up together.

The scary things not only happen in nature, but also human behavior.

That is when I realized, maybe, nature, maybe life,

was not beautiful as I imagined.

Junya Hatta

HERE.

To avoid being broken, I built the walls
with the "hardest" things I knew:
Bitterness and resentment.
So, I became impenetrable and that's how my life went.

But then I met you.
You were different.

For all these years, I have hidden behind a wall no one could see,
A hardened version of the child I used to be.
The one that believed in magic, in nature, in the beauty,
Instead of the death and destruction that I thought always pursued me.

You took my hand and led me to a field,
Where we sat surrounded by dandelions all around.
The ones that were once yellow
slowly turning to whisps of white like a cloud,
You picked one up, closed your eyes, blew them to the wind.
You said, "It's true that all beautiful things will die,
But from time to time,
You will be surprised,
Sometimes they come back, somewhere else, ready to thrive."

Junya Hatta

HERE.

I sat in mindless in silence. Then I reached for her hand.
She grabbed onto mine.
I looked into her eyes and said, "Sometimes 'life' happens,
But I guess,
so does the divine."

HERE.

I would rather risk boldly in the name of love.

Than to live a life of inaction.

Junya Hatta

HBD

Every day is my birthday,

for I was dead for the night and reborn in the morning.

For the me I was yesterday is dead and gone,

but I am here today to carry on.

Whatever yesterday was is no more,

what today will be is up to me to explore.

What tomorrow will be, I will never know

and I am okay with the uncertainty that comes with being born.

I am happy to be one day older and one day closer to another rebirth,

365 birthdays a year is how my mind should work.

Therefore, today, like all birthdays, is a celebration.

I will share this moment with the ones I love,

My life – appreciation.

Junya Hatta

GOOD AT GOODBYES

From time to time, we put our heart on the line,
loving people who may never love us back.
But in the process maybe in the love that we sowed,
maybe something beautiful will grow
and love will take root and hold,
giving hope to their life that didn't exist before.
Maybe we will never see the fruits of our labor,
but someday, someone else will reap the beauty
that never could have happened without us
and without our loving nature.

Junya Hatta

LEONA LEWIS

Maybe life is not easy

because you care too deeply.

You open hearts and it keeps on bleeding.

But I want you to know,

It may not show,

But your love is exactly what the world is needing.

HERE.

I WANT TO BE POOR WITH YOU PT. IV

We missed the final bus, so we started walking in the rain,
When she said, "Tell me some poems along the way."
So I did and she replied, "I could listen to your words for days."
But it was her that made this moment,
Poetically beyond anything I could say.

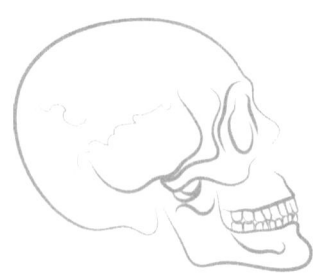

Junya Hatta

I WANT TO BE POOR WITH YOU PT. V

We laid on the floor for hours about her dreams,
Like how once she gets a real job, life will be better than it seems.
We can pay rent in a neighborhood close to a park,
where it's not so scary especially after dark.
Then she can go back to school to become a teacher,
Because she feels the kids really need her.
As she kept going, she started to drift asleep.
So I picked her up and then carried her to bed,
For both of us to dream.

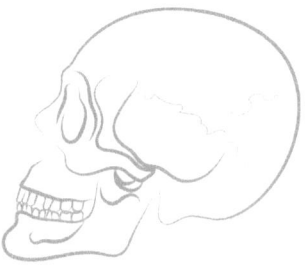

Junya Hatta

HERE.

LEAVES LEAVE THE TREE

I wonder how the leaves know,

when it's time to hold on and when it's time to let go.

When it's time to grow, to glow, and time to fall

to the ground below?

Something in their nature,

something in nature,

must dictate their behavior.

And I secretly wish, I knew just like the leaves,

when I should hold on and when to let go of the things,

that are a part of me.

Junya Hatta

INGRID

You came off free like on the wings of insects

Like blown by the morning breeze.

Your lyre voice nestled into the ears of mine.

The gentle curves of your smile,

Sliding into my mind.

No, we never matched,

But we were perfect.

By fate's flawed design.

Junya Hatta

BLESSINGS

I hold onto you, because from the start I always knew.
I felt like we met in a past life,
Like how two seeds of the same flower fell to the ground,
Grew up and we came to be around.
Our mere existence and through persistence,
somehow our paths crossed,
And we continued to hold onto the little hope we got,
No matter how much we seemed to be lost.
So now I believe what's meant to be must be,
And we are here, you and me.
The epitome of things working out,
Even if they don't work perfectly.
So deep down, I know we share the same roots.
Holding onto each other knowing love works,
Because we are living proof.

HERE.

SLOW DANCING IN A BURNING ROOM

I loved her angels for they danced with my demons.

I never wanted love,

Until she was exactly what I was needing.

HERE.

The weight of the world on one's shoulders,
can be carried with the weight of love in one's heart.

HERE.

I would have loved to be perfect.

Now it seems love has perfected me.

HERE.

WEST PENDER

At 2am I love to go home,

Where no one knows,

I fall apart.

Coming back from another night,

I think to myself, "Is this life?"

And, "Why is it so hard?"

Yes,

These nights are sad, yet somehow, I find them elegant,

And almost heaven sent.

Because when the world sleeps,

I get to be me where no one can see.

To a certain degree,

I can be free to be a little more me,

Whatever that means.

I love the quiet and tranquil,

How time is at a standstill.

And I pray for more 2am nights going home,

Alone.

Junya Hatta

HERE.

GO DEEP

Love is a boomerang.

Throw harder.

To reach farther.

Knowing, it will return.

Junya Hatta

HERE.

I found the greatest satisfaction
when I stopped looking
to get the most out of life and started
giving the most out of love.

Junya Hatta

HERE.

THE HURT THAT FEELS SO GOOD –
THE GOOD THAT FEELS LIKE HURT

Healing hurts

- as it always has -

as it always should

HERE.

Autumn is proof that Mother Nature is an artist.
The seasons her palette.
The world her canvas.

Junya Hatta

A LONG WAY HOME AT THE END OF THE ROAD

The irony of life is that,

It's the ups, downs, turn arounds,

The crossroads, off roads, forks in the roads,

Stop lights and off sights,

Beaten paths and vast unforeseen tracks,

give life direction.

HERE.

I wish for myself to fall in love once.

Maybe twice.

So, I learn how happy I can be through sacrifice.

| HERE.

Someone with the largest smile could only
have come from the greatest pain.
Because
someone already soaked doesn't mind
dancing in the rain.

Junya Hatta

HERE.

A ROSE IS A ROSE EVEN IF
IT DOESN'T LOOK LIKE A ROSE

When is a rose a rose?

When it's planted as a seed? Or when it grows?

When is a rose a rose?

I guess. All throughout I suppose?

A rose is a rose not from the petals or root,

But the process of transforming into something new.

Junya Hatta

HERE.

ALFRED

Love is the song

where I don't know the words,

but can hum along.

HERE.

We crave for beauty then kill it,

like when we see a flower and pick it.

So, let beauty be. Let it be free.

So, beauty can remain beautiful for everyone to see.

Junya Hatta

HERE.

My life is made from small, imperfect moments.

Stringed onto the chain of life.

They don't gleam in the light,

They don't draw one's attention.

But each point, my own.

They aren't diamonds and they aren't pearls from the sea.

Yet these memories are beautiful to me.

Junya Hatta

HERE.

TODAY IS THE DAY

Today

is a terrible thing

to waste.

HERE.

Somewhere in this dark time I will be there

with a pebble of love - thrown into a pool of life.

May the ripples extend to the far reaches of your soul.

Junya Hatta

HERE.

THE ROOT

What I learned is that the root of both fear and happiness come from the same source: the unknown. Fear is when the unknown causes us to imagine a result worse than what we are experiencing. Happiness on the other hand is the expectation of something better than the now. But both come from our incredible gift of imagination/expectation.

.

I hate people that tell me to be positive. I also hate people that tell me expect the worse. I feel it's somewhere in the middle (yet I'm not sure where in the middle) and in the process of finding this middle, I have found something I didn't expect: peace.

.

I feel peace is some balance of happiness and fear. Some joy in life to sustain you through the hardships, yet some fear to tread with caution and calculate risk. So in the process of trying to find a way "home", I've found a place within me to rest for the time being.

Junya Hatta

HERE.

Maybe this crazy world doesn't need sane answers,

But just as crazy type of love.

Junya Hatta

HERE.

Maybe we are obsessed with beautiful stories,
Because somewhere, deep down inside of us,
We have one of our own waiting to be lived out.

Junya Hatta

HERE.

I used to fear the rain.

Now I only fear missing the rainbow that remains.

Junya Hatta

HERE.

There is no such thing as a love story,

for all stories have an end.

Love is therefore,

poetry,

for it flows forever waiting for you to swim in

again and again.

Junya Hatta

KNOW ME

I would love for you to know me in a deep and intimate way.
I know it's hard to explain, that is why I want you
to meet me in a whole new way.
I want to know your existence through my existence,
Where you living adds life to mine,
Where your presence is felt and your absence
a constant reminder of my demise.
Like the way the flower knows the sun by blooming,
like the way it knows the rain by growing its roots.
But as soon as one disappears, then it withers or drowns.
You being around has an effect so profound,
I realize,
my future depends on things beyond my control,
so here I am,
rain on me,
shine on me,
know me,
and make me grow.

Junya Hatta

HERE.

She asked, "What is love?"

He said, "I don't know, but you're the only one I want to figure it out with."

I'M HERE

One upon a time, in the world of Verb,
Lived many heroes, who were superiorly superb.

They were the best heroes, in all the world,
Bringing happiness to, little boys and girls.

The heroes were special, in their own little way,
For each had a power, that saved the day.

For example,
There was Give, who gave children candies and toys.
Because gifts make us happy! Especially little girls and boys.

Oh and then there was Play!
He used games and fun to save the day.

And finally, there was Work! She helped you achieve,
Your smallest and biggest goals, to always succeed.

Those were the four...Did I just say four?
Oops I forgot, there was one more...

Junya Hatta

HERE.

Ah yes...the last one, his name was Here.
Yes, "Here".
What was his super power? He always showed up,
but what he did? No one was clear.

But anyways it doesn't matter,
Because Here couldn't do anything,
for he was simply a disaster.

But Here was determined to one day be,
The greatest superhero for you and me.

One day, there was a cry for help,
"My chance," thought Here, "I'll save her myself!"

"Mister, he stole my doll and won't give it back.
Can you please help? I'm feeling terribly sad."

Although Here was first on the scene,
but didn't know what to say,
Then came Give, with gifts to give away.

"Here little girl. A brand-new doll!
Don't thank me, it's nothing at all!"

Junya Hatta

HERE.

"Thanks..." as she stuttered to say,
"My name is Give and I give gifts all day!"

The little girl and Give walked back to her home,
Leaving Here at the scene, standing all alone.

Here felt like he wasn't a hero,
Then he heard a voice, faint, but near though.

"Uuughhhh I'm so lonely..." a voice stated,
"Another chance!" Here was elated!

"I have no one to play with, no one at all.
Can you play catch? I'll throw you the ball!"

The little boy threw the ball and to Here's surprise,
He caught it! Even though he closed his eyes.

He cheered and Here was so proud,
"Throw it back to me!" the boy yelled out loud.

Here pulled back and threw it as hard as he could,

HERE.

"Whoosh!" but the ball landed right by his foot.

"You throw like a wussy," the little boy said.
"I want someone else to play with me instead."

Just then, Play appeared from the sky,
"Don't worry little boy! I'm your type of guy!"

He picked up the ball and threw it so hard,
Yet, it landed so softly into the little boy's arms.

"Great throw Play! You have quite the arm!"
"Great catch little boy!" Play shouted with charm.

As the little boy and Play continued their game,
Here was feeling, deeply ashamed.

Just then,
Another voice, out in the distance,
"Arrgghh I don't understand! I need help this instant!"

"Another chance!" thought Here to himself,
Now I can finally be a hero and be of some help!

Junya Hatta

HERE.

Here was first on the scene and frantically looked,
And saw a little girl up to her noses in books!

He knew exactly what a hero would do,
"I brought you a toy and some candy for you!"

"I don't need a toy!" she snarled at Here.
"I need help with homework. Do I make myself clear?!"

"No worries," thought Here for he knew
something else a hero would do,
"I have a ball I can play catch with you!"

"Catch!?!? No, no, no! I don't have time!
I can't go to college if I'm falling behind!"

Here felt stumped, "But you're so young..."
"But I'm already nine and applications have begun!"

Just then, "Whoosh!", Here felt a gust,
"My name is Work! And I guarantee an A+!"

The little girl's eyes started to glimmer,

Junya Hatta

HERE.

As Work taught thermodynamics,
But of course, made it simpler.

Here sighed and stated,
"It's very clear though…
I'll never be a hero."

Just then, Here heard a sound,
Spun in circles and looked around.

There was a man sitting on some steps,
With his face in his hands looking very upset.

Not only was Here, first at the scene,
But also Give, Play, and Work came after to work as a team.

"Here don't get in the way.
Let us REAL heroes save the day."

"My name is Give and here's something dandy.
Everyone loves…toys and candy!"

The man didn't look up, but continued to sob,

Toys and candy, couldn't make him stop.

"My name is Play and here's something neat!
We can play catch...or Hide and Seek!"

The man didn't look up, but continued to sob,
Playing games couldn't make him stop.

"My name is Work and here's something you need!
I'll teach you investing to help you succeed!"

The man didn't look up, but continued to sob,
Work or success, couldn't make him stop.

Then, Here walked up and sat by the man,
Put his arms around him...
"What is he doing?" said Give, "I don't understand!!"

The man looked up and wiped his eyes,
"Who are you?" he said looking surprised.

"I'm Here."

Junya Hatta

HERE.

"Sorry? Are you a superhero too? Who are you again?
And what're you trying to do my friend?"

"I'm not trying to do anything. I'm just Here."

The sobbing man smiled and put his arms around Here.
"Thank you. I appreciate you just being near."

Here helped the man walk back home,
Leaving Give, Play, and Work standing all alone.

Junya Hatta

The End.

follow along for more words & poetry

@junya_hatta

www.ingramcontent.com/pod-product-compliance
Lightning Source LLC
Chambersburg PA
CBHW030313100526
44590CB00012B/625